I Wonder Why

Whales Sing

and Other Questions About Sea Life

Caroline Harris

KINGFISHER

KINGFISHER

First published in 2006 by Kingfisher
an imprint of Macmillan Children's Books
a division of Macmillan Publishers Limited
The Macmillan Building, 4 Crinan Street,
London N1 9XW
Basingstoke and Oxford
Associated companies throughout the world
www.panmacmillan.com

ISBN 978-0-7534-1292-3

Copyright © Macmillan Children's Books 2006

9 8 7 6 5 4 3 2 1
1TR/1008/SHENS/HBM/126.6MA/F

A CIP catalogue record is available for this book from the British Library.

Printed in Taiwan

Illustrations: Marin Camm 4–5, 8–9, 10–11, 14–15, 16–17, 20–21, 22–23,
26–27, 30–31; Michael Langham Rowe 6–7, 12–13, 18–19, 24–25, 28–29.
Peter Wilks (SGA) all cartoons.

CONTENTS

4 Why do fish not drown?

5 Why do divers need headlights?

5 Where does grass grow under water?

6 Which animal swims by waving?

6 Why are octopuses like jet planes?

7 Why does a fish need fins?

8 Which fish uses a rod to catch food?

8 What uses combs for eating?

9 What looks like a flower but is really a trap?

10 Which crab borrows its house?

10 Which shellfish digs with its foot?

11 Why do some fish have their eyes on their side?

12 Why are lionfish like porcupines?

12 Which fish wears armour?

13 What hides in ink?

14 Why do baby dolphins need guards?

15 What jumps up waterfalls?

15 What is busy at full moon?

16 Where can you see smoke?

17 What are sponges?

17 Which animals march in line?

18 Which is the brainiest part of the ocean?

19 What lettuce would make a nasty sandwich?

19 What has a funny home?

20 Why do whales sing?

20 What is spyhopping?

21 What causes strandings?

22 How do dolphins stand up?

22 What is like an elephant?

23 How do seals and sealions keep warm?

24 How do sharks find their food?

24 What is strange about a shark's skeleton?

25 What use is a long tail?

25 How dangerous are sharks?

26 Which fish has binoculars?

27 What looks like the night sky?

27 When is a spider not a spider?

28 Which bird hangs its wings to dry?

28 Why do crabs run sideways?

29 Which lizard goes swimming?

30 What is whale-watching?

31 How can satellites help sea creatures?

31 Who cleans beaches?

Why do fish not drown?

Humans can't breathe in water, but fish can. Oxygen is found in water as well as in the air. To breathe, fish gulp in water. Instead of lungs, they have red, frilly flaps called gills on each side of their head.

gill slit

● When water flows over the gills, the oxygen in it passes into the fish's blood. Long, curved slits let the water out.

● A glass of sea water is full of minerals called salts, and millions of tiny plants and animals known as plankton.

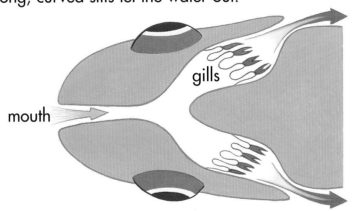

gills

mouth

● At 30 metres long and weighing up to 190 tonnes, the blue whale is the biggest animal on Earth. It's as long as 18 men swimming in a line, head to toe. But its favourite dish, a shrimp-like animal called krill, is tiny. It measures just a few centimetres.

● All land animals are descended from sea creatures. Millions of years ago, the first animals crept out of the water to start life on land.

Why do divers need headlights?

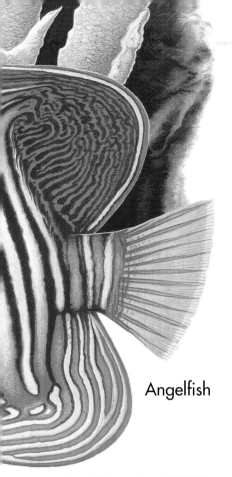

Angelfish

Only the first 200 metres below the surface of the ocean are lit by the sun. This is where all sea plants and most sea animals live. Below that is the murky twilight zone. The midnight zone, from 1,000 metres down, is totally dark.

Sunlight zone

200 metres

Twilight zone

Midnight zone

Abyssal zone

Dugong

Sea grass

Where does grass grow under water?

Sea grass grows in shallow water and is the only ocean plant that has flowers. In warm waters, dugongs graze on it. Dugongs are also known as sea cows.

● Life on Earth began in the seas, more than 3,500 million years ago. People have found fossils of the ancient animals.

Which animal swims by waving?

Rays have wide, strong side fins that make them look like underwater kites. The ray's muscles make these fins move in a wave. The ripple begins at the front, where the fins join the head, and travels along to the back, pushing the ray through the water. Rays are flat, and often glide along near the sea floor – but their closest cousins are sharks!

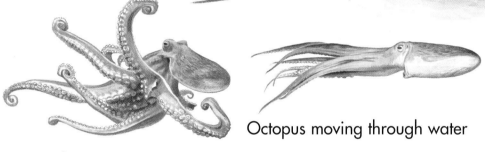

Octopus moving through water

Why are octopuses like jet planes?

Octopuses, squid, cuttlefish and scallops all use jet propulsion to zip through the sea. Octopuses pump water in over their gills and squirt it out through a fleshy tube called a siphon. They can point the siphon in almost any direction, which helps them to steer.

● The by-the-wind sailor jellyfish has a flat sail that it holds at an angle to the wind. It is blown across the ocean surface, like a sailing boat.

● Starfish crawl along on thousands of tube feet. Each one has to reach forwards in the direction the starfish wants to move.

Manta ray

● Turtles are reptiles, but instead of four legs, they have flat flippers. The turtle beats the front pair like wings to 'fly' through the water.

● Some types of fish can 'walk'. Batfish have a pair of long, thick fins underneath their body. They use these to creep over the ocean bottom.

Why does a fish need fins?

Fish use their fins to power them along, and for balance, steering, braking and swimming backwards. Fish wriggle through the water, a bit like a snake, but they also swish their tail fins for added speed. Other fins help them to keep level.

Which fish uses a rod to catch food?

The anglerfish has a long spine on its head with a bobble, or lure, on the end that it shakes to attract smaller fish – like someone with a fishing rod. The lures of deep-sea anglerfish even glow, so they can catch fish in the dark.

● Electric rays and stargazer fish are among the 250 types that can give the animals they hunt a nasty electric shock. They have special organs that work like batteries.

Anglerfish

Ray

What uses combs for eating?

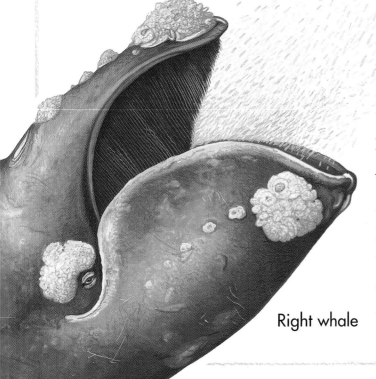
Right whale

Many of the largest whales are filter feeders, and eat by pushing water through rows of tightly packed plates in their mouths. Plankton and small fish get caught in the combs, called baleen, and can be swallowed.

lure

● Tiny cleaner fish dart into the mouths of sharks and other fish and feed on scraps of food caught in their teeth. Luckily for the cleaner fish, the sharks don't eat their living toothbrushes!

● The jaws of the gulper eel open so wide it can swallow a fish much larger than itself. It needs to grab any fish that pass by as food is hard to find deep in the sea.

What looks like a flower but is really a trap?

Sea anemones are named after a flower because at high tide their tentacles open up like petals. But shrimps or small fish that brush past these 'flowers' get a nasty sting. This stuns the fish, so the anemone can eat them.

Which crab borrows its house?

Most crabs are protected by a hard casing all over, but the hermit crab is a bit of a softy. Its shell is very thin, so it needs something tougher to make a safe home. It finds an empty shell, backs into it and walks away with a new house.

Which shellfish digs with its foot?

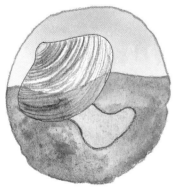

Many types of clam burrow into the seabed, and then stay there. They have a strong 'foot' made of muscle that pulls them down into the sand. A clam's shell has two halves, which it can close up tight if it is threatened.

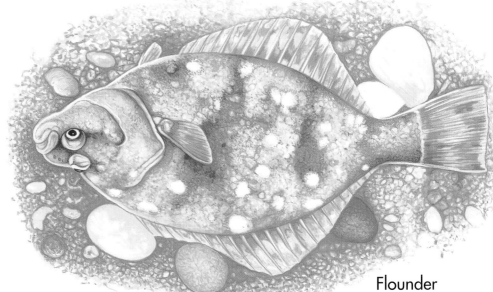

Flounder

● Cuttlefish fool any animals that want to eat them by changing colour and pattern. They do this to match the part of the seabed they are swimming over.

Why do some fish have their eyes on their side?

Flatfish, such as plaice, sole and flounder, lie on their sides on the seabed to hide from enemies. The 'side' that is on top becomes coloured to match the ocean floor. One eye also moves around to this side, so it won't be buried in the mud.

● Sargassum fish look like seaweed, but don't be fooled. These fish aren't shy and retiring – they are fierce fighters.

● Tower shells and mussels are molluscs. These creatures have soft bodies but can build hard shells around themselves.

Tower shell

Mussel

● Decorator crabs drape their shells with seaweed and sponges. It might not be high fashion, but it helps them hide from enemies.

Why are lionfish like porcupines?

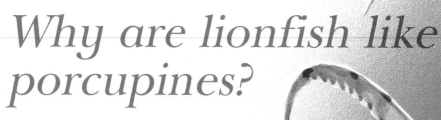

From a distance, a lionfish looks as though it has a mane. But up close, you'll find this fish's prickles are more deadly than its bite. When an enemy shows up, the lionfish spreads out its fins to show off its long spines. Anything that swims too near risks being speared!

● The Australian box jellyfish is more dangerous than a cobra. Its venom can kill a person in a few minutes.

Which fish wears armour?

With plenty of hungry sea animals ready to gobble them up, smaller creatures need to carry protection. In place of ordinary scales, the boxfish is covered with six-sided bony plates, fused together to make stiff armour. Only its mouth, eyes and fins can move freely.

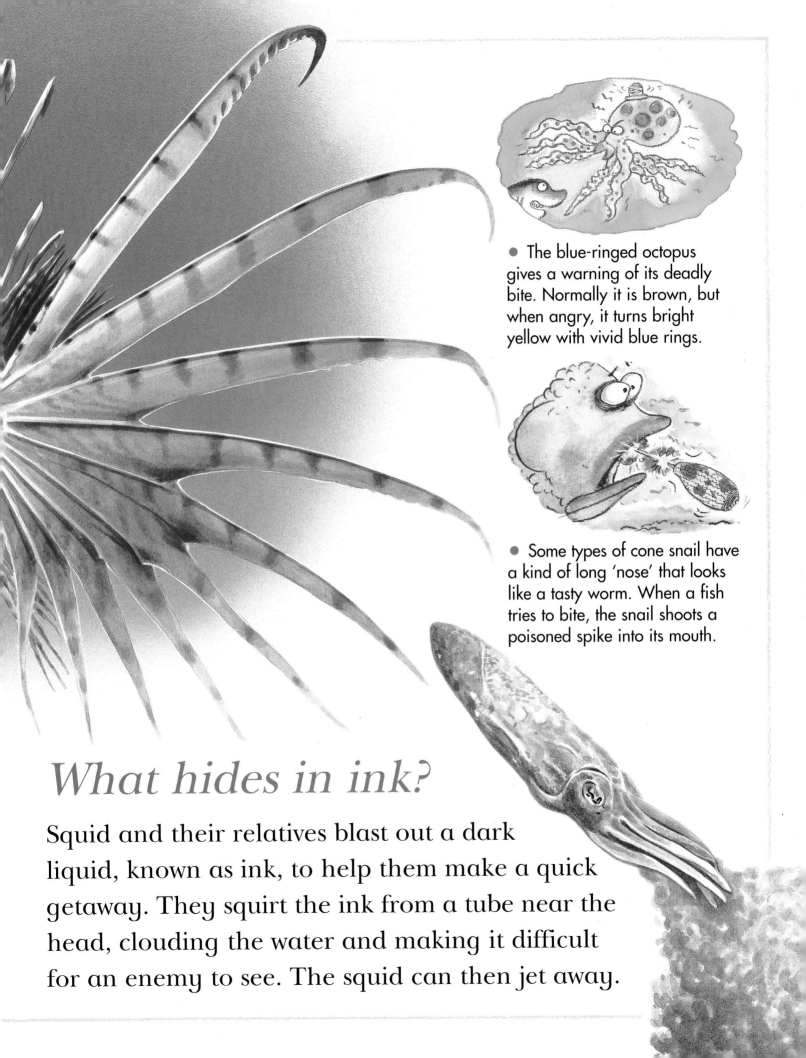

● The blue-ringed octopus gives a warning of its deadly bite. Normally it is brown, but when angry, it turns bright yellow with vivid blue rings.

● Some types of cone snail have a kind of long 'nose' that looks like a tasty worm. When a fish tries to bite, the snail shoots a poisoned spike into its mouth.

What hides in ink?

Squid and their relatives blast out a dark liquid, known as ink, to help them make a quick getaway. They squirt the ink from a tube near the head, clouding the water and making it difficult for an enemy to see. The squid can then jet away.

Why do baby dolphins need guards?

A young dolphin, called a calf, has to be protected all the time from sharks and other enemies. If the mother has to leave her calf to find food, other females guard the baby from enemies.

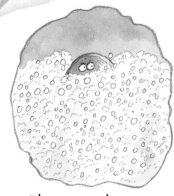

● Blue mussels produce an incredible 12 million eggs at a time. A lot won't survive, but with so many eggs, thousands will still hatch.

● Orcas can live in their family group, known as a pod, for the whole of their life. They are also called killer whales, but orcas are really large dolphins and do not harm humans.

● Jawfish dads take parenting seriously. They store the female's eggs in their mouths to keep them safe until the eggs hatch. When he eats, the male puts the eggs in his burrow.

What jumps up waterfalls?

Atlantic salmon spend most of their life at sea, but swim back to the river where they were born when it's time to breed. They battle against the flow of the river, and some even have to leap up waterfalls.

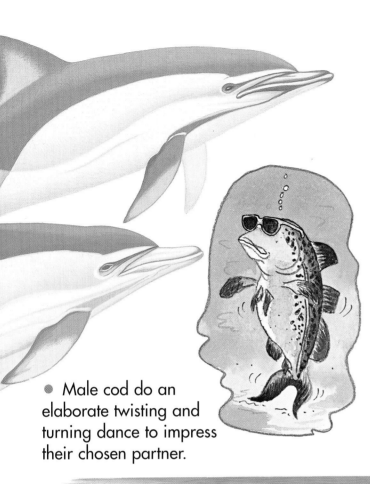

● Male cod do an elaborate twisting and turning dance to impress their chosen partner.

What is busy at full moon?

In spring, on nights when the moon is full, thousands of horseshoe crabs make their way up beaches along the Pacific and on the east coast of the USA to lay their eggs. At the next full moon, the baby horseshoe crabs hatch out and return to the sea.

Where can you see smoke?

Cracks in the deep ocean floor spew out water that has been heated in the Earth's crust. The water can reach 450°C – twice as hot as most ovens. It contains particles from the rocks it has passed through, which appear as billowing clouds of smoke.

● Piddocks tunnel into rocks by twisting around, so their rough front end drills into the stone. They never leave their self-made caves.

● Sea pens, which are related to jellyfish, look like an old-fashioned quill pen. Add some squid ink and you could write an underwater letter!

What are sponges?

Most bath sponges are now made from plastic, but natural sponges are the skeletons of living seabed creatures. Sponges are very simple animals. They collect tiny bits of food by pumping water through their bodies.

● Sea mice have gold fur and live in burrows. But they aren't mice at all – they're worms. They live in shallow water and push themselves through the sand and mud.

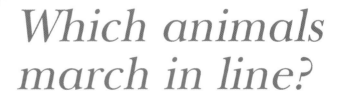

Which animals march in line?

Spiny lobsters walk along the ocean floor one after the other on their five pairs of legs. The line can be 60 lobsters long, and they sometimes travel 15 kilometres a day. Each one keeps in touch with the lobster in front by using its feelers, or antennae.

Which is the brainiest part of the ocean?

Coral reefs are home to corals of all shapes and sizes. They are made by millions of animals, called polyps, which build stony skeletons. When the polyps die the skeletons are left behind, and the living coral makes a new layer on top.

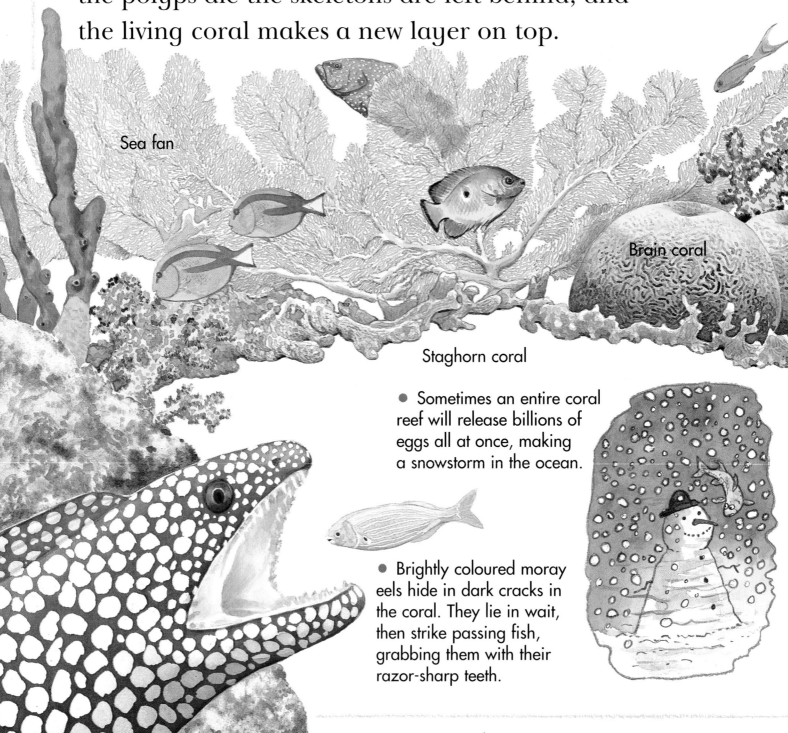

Sea fan

Brain coral

Staghorn coral

● Sometimes an entire coral reef will release billions of eggs all at once, making a snowstorm in the ocean.

● Brightly coloured moray eels hide in dark cracks in the coral. They lie in wait, then strike passing fish, grabbing them with their razor-sharp teeth.

What lettuce would make a nasty sandwich?

A lettuce slug may look like a crunchy leaf, but this is a disguise to fool enemies. The sea slugs that live on reefs are as colourful as the fish. This is often a warning that they taste bad or are poisonous to eat.

Tubular sponge

• Coral reefs face many dangers. Some fishermen use dynamite to kill fish and this damages the reefs. They are also eaten by crown-of-thorns starfish.

What has a funny home?

The clownfish is one of the many bright coral reef fish. It lives in the stinging tentacles of a sea anemone, but isn't hurt because its skin is covered with slimy mucus, which protects it. The clownfish is safe from attack, and the anemone can feast on its leftovers.

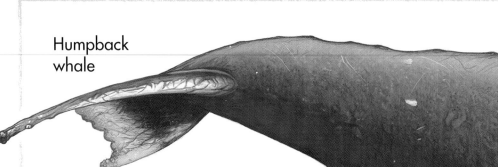

Humpback
whale

Why do whales sing?

Whales are talkative animals. They bellow, grunt, yelp and make bubbling noises to find other whales and send messages. Male humpback whales sing long tunes, sometimes repeating them for hours or days. This is probably to attract a mate.

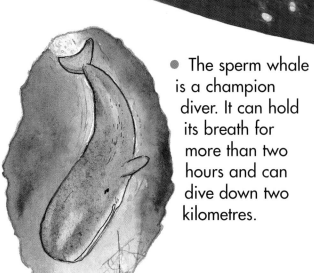

● The sperm whale is a champion diver. It can hold its breath for more than two hours and can dive down two kilometres.

What is spyhopping?

Because whales and dolphins are mammals – like you – they have to breathe air, so are often seen on the surface. Spyhopping is when they stick their heads straight out of the water, often to look for food such as seals resting on the ice.

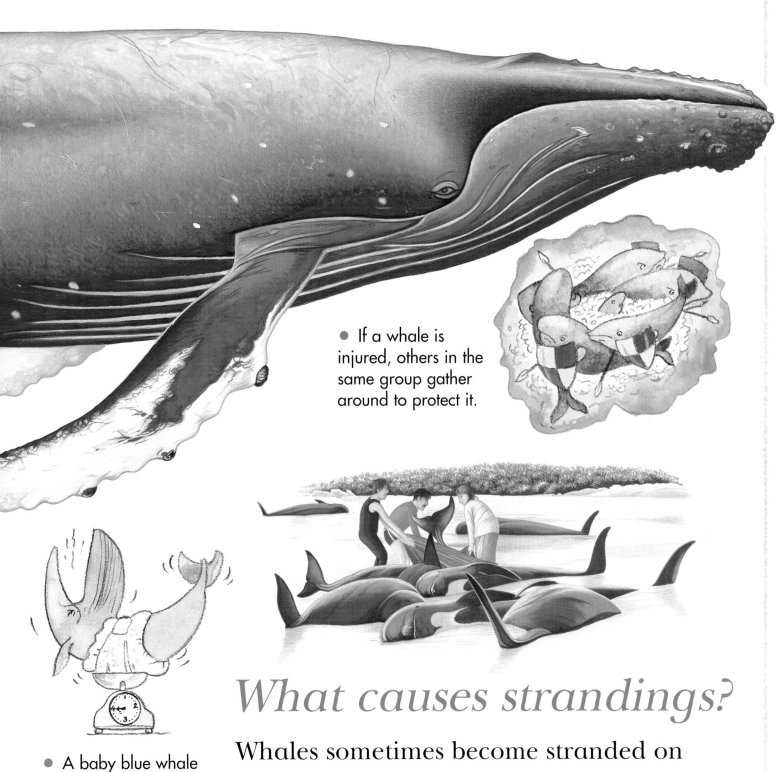

● If a whale is injured, others in the same group gather around to protect it.

What causes strandings?

Whales sometimes become stranded on beaches. No one knows why they do it, but people can help save their lives by keeping them damp and making sure their blowholes are free of sand and water so that they can breathe.

● A baby blue whale weighs four tonnes at birth – the same as an adult hippo or a medium-sized truck – and is eight metres long. The next biggest baby is the fin whale, which weighs two tonnes.

How do dolphins stand up?

A dolphin's tail is very powerful. It is so strong that dolphins can leap right out of the sea and stay standing up. The tail moves up and down, not side to side like a fish. Its sweep pushes the dolphin through the water.

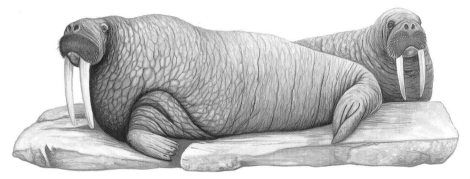

What is like an elephant?

Walruses have leathery skin and tusks, similar to an elephant's, that can be nearly a metre long. These tusks are extra-large upper teeth that grow throughout their life.

● At five metres long, male elephant seals are the giants of the seal world. They spend most of their lives at sea, and come to shore only to find a mate.

● From a distance, and in the moonlight when they like to feed, manatees or dugongs can look strangely human. In the past, they have been mistaken for mermaids!

How do seals and sealions keep warm?

Many sea mammals have a thick layer of fat, called blubber, beneath their skin to keep the heat in. Some seals and sealions have hair, and others have thick furry coats with a second layer of shorter hair near the skin to keep the water out.

● Sea otters use their tummies as tables, and rocks to prepare their food. They carry stones to the sea surface and crush the shells of sea urchins, lobsters, crabs and clams with them.

How do sharks find their food?

Sharks use six senses to find their next meal. They see better than humans do, and can sniff out blood in the water hundreds of metres away. They can also sense the small amounts of electricity that are given off by all living things.

● Sharks aren't fussy eaters. They swallow whatever they can find in the sea, including tin cans, leather jackets and even a bottle of wine!

What is strange about a shark's skeleton?

Most fish skeletons are bony, but a shark's is made of cartilage. This is the springy stuff that gives your nose and ears their shape. Shark skin is covered with tooth-like scales that make it as rough as sandpaper.

What use is a long tail?

The thresher shark's tail is almost as long as its body. The shark whips its tail from side to side to herd fish into a group. The force of the lashes also stuns the fish, so the thresher can snap them up with its strong teeth.

● The nurse shark grows a new set of teeth every week. Other sharks have extra rows of teeth in case some wear out.

How dangerous are sharks?

Most species of shark aren't dangerous to humans, and eat only tiny plankton and fish. Some shark attacks on people might be a case of mistaken identity. Surfers can look like seals from under the water, and some sharks snack on these sea mammals.

Which fish has binoculars?

Some weird creatures live in the deep ocean. Gigantura has tube-shaped eyes with bulging lenses that look like binoculars. These help it spot even the faintest glow from its prey. Hatchetfish have strange eyes that can only look upwards.

Hatchetfish

Gigantura

Viperfish

Black dragon

● At 5,000 metres, the pressure of the water is so great it would crush your body. But animals have to live, swim and eat here!

● No one has ever seen a fully grown adult colossal squid, but scientists reckon it would be more than 18 metres long.

● The tripod fish spends most of its life standing around. It perches on three thin fins, and waits for its dinner to bump into it.

Anglerfish

Lanternfish

● Red opossum
shrimps spurt out
liquid that bursts
into clouds of light.
This confuses any
fish that fancy
them for supper.

What looks like the night sky?

Lanternfish are dotted with small shining spots, so they look like clusters of stars swimming along. But they're not alone – most deep ocean animals can make their own light. This helps them to recognize each other in the dark!

When is a spider not a spider?

Sea spiders are cousins of the land variety, but are a separate kind, called pycnogonids. Sea spiders don't scuttle, but creep on their spindly legs so they don't stir up the slimy goo on the seabed.

Which bird hangs its wings to dry?

Cormorants dive into the ocean to catch eels and fish, then come ashore and perch on a rock, holding out their wings. Their feathers do not have the waterproofing oils that cover most sea birds, so they need to be dried by the sun and breeze.

● Eiders are sea ducks that live on rocky coasts and enjoy crab for supper. Quilts used to be filled with their fluffy feathers.

● Most starfish have five arms or a multiple of five, such as ten or 20. If one of the arms gets broken off, the starfish grows another!

Why do crabs run sideways?

Crabs have their skeletons on the outside, as a hard shell that covers their bodies. Most can walk any way they want, but the leg joints of some crabs move in only one direction, like your knee or elbow. So it's easiest to scuttle.

- Emperor penguins balance their eggs on their feet, and protect them from the Antarctic chill with a built-in 'egg-cosy'.

Which lizard goes swimming?

The marine iguana, found in the Galapagos islands, is the only sea lizard. It swims underwater to eat seaweed but must quickly do some sunbathing after a dip in the cold sea. It is cold-blooded and needs the sun to warm it up.

- Cowrie shells have been used as money in more places around the world than any coin! In the past you could buy and sell with them in countries from India to the USA.

- The frigate bird, which soars over tropical seas, has a bright red neck pouch that it blows up like a balloon. It does this to show off to females.

What is whale-watching?

Many tourists now go on boat trips to watch whales in their natural surroundings. This helps people understand more about these special creatures, and makes sure the places where they live are kept safe.

● Throughout history, sailors have told tales of terrifying sea monsters. But we now know that most of these monsters are ordinary sea creatures.

● Some fishing boats drag huge nets through the water, catching lots of fish. But this has made some fish very rare, and may damage the ocean floor.

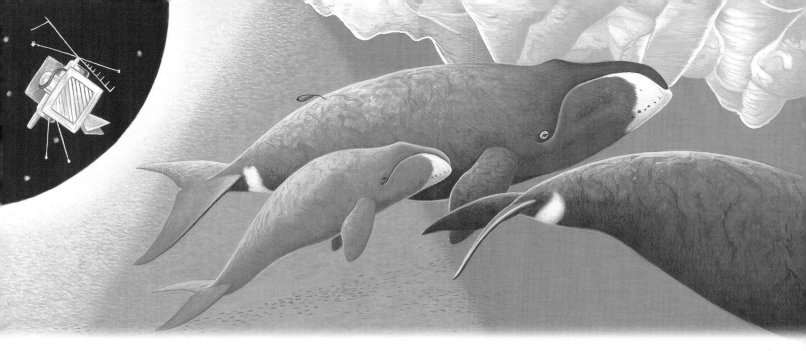

How can satellites help sea creatures?

Special tags attached to bowhead whales and other sea animals send a signal to satellites in space. This allows scientists to track where the whales go, and helps us learn more about them. We can then protect them better.

● Purple dye, made by crushing lots of tiny sea snails, was used to colour the robes of ancient kings.

● In Japan, puffer fish is an expensive treat – but if you eat the wrong parts, the fish's poison will kill you!

Who cleans beaches?

Sometimes sticky oil spills out of ships that carry it, polluting the sea and beaches. It poisons sea creatures and can kill them. Teams of people clean up the beaches to save the animals' lives.

Index

A

anglerfish 8
Atlantic salmon 15

B

baleen 8
batfish 7
blubber 23
boxfish 12

C

cartilage 24
clams 10
cleaner fish 9
clownfish 19
cone snails 13
coral reefs 18
cormorants 28
cowrie shells 29
crabs 10, 11, 15, 23, 28
cuttlefish 6, 11

D

dolphins 14, 15, 22, 23
dugongs 5, 23

E

eels 18, 28
eggs 14, 15, 18, 29
eiders 28
electric rays 8
elephant seals 22
emperor penguins 29

F

fins 6, 7, 12, 26
flatfish 11
frigate birds 29

G

giganturas 26
gills 4, 6
gulper eels 9

H

hatchetfish 26

J

jawfish 14
jellyfish 6, 12, 16

K

krill 4

L

lanternfish 27
lettuce slugs 19
lionfish 12, 13

M

manatees 23
marine iguanas 29
mussels 14

O

octopuses 6, 13
oil spills 31
orcas 14

P

piddocks 16
plankton 4, 8, 25
polyps 18
puffer fish 31

R

rays 6, 8

S

sargassum fish 11
satellites 31
scientists 4, 26, 31
sea anemones 9, 19
sea cows see dugongs
sea grass 5
sea mice 17
sea otters 23
sea pens 16
sea spiders 27
sea urchins 23
sealions 23
seals 20, 22, 23, 25
seaweed 11, 29
sharks 6, 9, 24, 25
shellfish 10
shells 10, 11, 29
shrimps 4, 9, 27
skeletons 17, 18, 24, 28
spiny lobsters 17
sponges 11, 17
spyhopping 20
squid 6, 13, 16, 26
starfish 7, 19
stargazer fish 8
strandings 21

T

teeth 9, 18, 22, 25
tentacles 9
tower shells 11
tripod fish 26
turtles 7

W

walruses 22
whales 4, 8, 14, 20–21, 30–31
whale-watching 30